To my
truest Love,
   Jeffery,
with all my heart;
      Joyce
   June 27th, 1992

The Green Thoreau

The
Green Thoreau

Selected and with an Introduction by
CAROL SPENARD LARUSSO

THE CLASSIC WISDOM COLLECTION
NEW WORLD LIBRARY
SAN RAFAEL, CALIFORNIA

The Classic Wisdom Collection
Published by New World Library
58 Paul Drive, San Rafael, CA 94903

Cover design: Greg Wittrock
Text design: Nancy Benedict
Typography: Wilsted & Taylor

Library of Congress Cataloging-in-Publication Data

Thoreau, Henry David, 1817–1862.
    The green Thoreau / selected, and with an introduction
by Carol Spenard LaRusso.
    p.   cm. — (The Classic wisdom collection)
  Includes bibliographical references.
ISBN 0-931432-93-6 (acid-free paper)
  1. Thoreau, Henry David, 1817–1862—Quotations.
2. Nature—Quotations, maxims, etc. I. LaRusso, Carol
Spenard, 1935– . II. Title. III. Series.
PS3042.L37 1992
818'.402—dc20   91-40224
                                                 CIP

First printing, April 1992
ISBN 0-931432-93-6
Printed in the U.S.A. on acid-free paper

*For my children and grandchildren
and all young life on our planet*

Contents

Publisher's Preface

Life is an endless cycle of change. We and our world will never remain the same.

Every generation has difficulty relating to the previous generation; even the language changes. The child speaks a different language than the parent.

It seems almost miraculous, then, that certain voices, certain books, are able to speak to not only one, but many generations beyond them. The plays and poems of William Shakespeare are still relevant today—still capable of giving us goose bumps, still entertaining, disturbing, and profound. Shakespeare is the writer who, in the English language, defines the word *classic*.

There are many other writers and thinkers who, for a great many reasons, can be considered classic, for they withstand the test of time. We want to present the best of them to you in the New World Library Classic Wisdom Collection, the thinkers who, even though they lived many years ago, are still relevant and important in today's world for the enduring words of wisdom they created, words that should forever be kept in print.

Shakti Gawain
Marc Allen
New World Library

Introduction

The words of Henry David Thoreau (1817–1862) sound with a deep resonance in the waning years of the twentieth century. One hundred and thirty years after his death, the clarity of his vision seems marked especially for our time. Thoreau, with his deep love of the natural world, used nature as his teacher, companion, and as a source of healing, renewal, and inspiration.

Though Thoreau's writings and message were largely ignored during his own lifetime and afterward as well, we no longer have the luxury of time in which to be similarly shortsighted. We are the first generations to experience the effects of exponential population explosion, rampant industrialism, myriad technological invention, dizzying social-political

xi

change, and climatic and environmental damage—all of which have dramatically altered our familiar planetary landscape within a few short decades.

Thoreau, probably the first environmentalist (long before that concept was ever formed), divined that "in wildness is the preservation of the world." These prophetic words serve as our wake-up call. Only recently we've learned how the systematic destruction of the rain forest has adversely affected the ecosystem of our fragile planet. In the face of many environmental and ethical difficulties we look around us for help. Not only do we need brilliant new technology to help solve the problems that our old technology created, we also need inspiration, vision, and guidance. In Thoreau's always eloquent and often lyrical prose, we find a nineteenth-century man so amazingly ahead of his time that most of us in the twentieth century have not yet caught up. He has much to teach us not only about the nurturing of our natural world, but also about the wise management of all our resources: our time, money, work, talents, health.

Thoreau believed in the freedom and potential of the individual, that each of us makes a difference in influencing our collective human life. Despite the power and proliferation of world governments, we have seen over and over again the incredible power of the individual and of the people—of grass roots movements that shape history. One of the most famous was influenced by Thoreau's essay, *On the Duty of Civil Disobedience*, which served as the primer for Gandhi's nonviolent resistance campaign in India. The civil rights movement led by Martin Luther King, Jr., was similarly influenced. Even the "second" Russian revolution in the Soviet Union in 1991 demonstrated the concept of passive resistance to an unjust government. Thoreau was not especially a political man, but was a man of courage who definitely "walked his talk." In 1846 he spent a night in the Concord, Massachusetts, jail for refusing to pay a poll tax to a government which supported slavery and the Mexican War.

But Thoreau, a freedom-loving individualist, would not want us to imitate him.

Rather, he demands that we examine how we spend our lives, and then work out our own salvation. Thoreau chose to build a cabin on the shores of Walden Pond and live there for over two years, not to escape society or to set an example, but to learn his life lessons: "I went to the woods because I wished to live deliberately, to front only the essential facts of life, and see if I could learn what it had to teach. . . ." Each of us will learn our life lessons in our own way—finding our own personal "Walden."

Our path ahead as citizens and custodians of planet Earth may be difficult. It could be that we must downshift and make some sacrifices in order to achieve other, more important goals. Much of what Thoreau says is not what we want to hear. He asks, "Shall we always study to obtain more of these things [possessions] and not sometimes to be content with less?" Or: "A man is rich in proportion to the number of things he can afford to let alone." Thoreau's compelling observations serve as catalysts for us to rethink our lives and discover how to live them with more integrity and wisdom. We could wander in the treasure trove of his thought indefinitely.

The Green Thoreau has been prepared both as a practical and an inspirational guide for our journey from the old century to a new one. I have selected illustrative passages from Thoreau's lesser-known essays and books (some of which were delivered as lectures and published posthumously), as well as from *Walden*, published in 1854. His artistry, passion, and vision inspire us to reach beyond our years and experience to more wisely face the challenges of a new millennium. Thoreau is there already— our best guide and teacher.

Carol Spenard LaRusso
Novato, California, 1992

A note on the text: We can interpret Thoreau's use of the words "man" and "men" to include women as well! Some outdated punctuation has been changed to reflect modern usage; for example, where a dash is preceded by a comma, the comma has been omitted, and obsolete hyphens have been eliminated from such words as "to-day" and "to-morrow." However, no changes have been made that would alter Thoreau's meaning or thought.

The Green Thoreau

1

Nature

"The earth is not a mere fragment of dead history, stratum upon stratum like the leaves of a book, to be studied by geologists and antiquaries chiefly, but living poetry like the leaves of a tree, which precede flowers and fruit—not a fossil earth, but a living earth."

WALDEN, *Spring*

This winter they are cutting down our woods more seriously than ever. Thank God, they cannot cut down the clouds!

JOURNAL, *January 21, 1852*

If a man walks in the woods for love of them half of each day, he is in danger of being regarded as a loafer; but if he spends his whole day as a speculator, shearing off those woods and making Earth bald before her time, he is esteemed an industrious and enterprising citizen. As if a town had no interest in its forests but to cut them down!

LIFE WITHOUT PRINCIPLE, *1863*

I wish to speak a word for Nature, for absolute freedom and wildness, as contrasted with a freedom and culture merely civil—to regard man as an inhabitant, or a part and parcel of Nature, rather than as a member of society.

Nowadays almost all man's improvements, so called, as the building of houses and the cutting down of the forest and of all large trees, simply deform the landscape, and make it more and more tame and cheap.

WALKING, *1862*

He who cuts down woods beyond a certain limit exterminates birds.

JOURNAL, *May 17, 1853*

When I consider that the nobler animals have been exterminated here—the cougar, the panther, the lynx, wolverine, wolf, bear, moose, the deer, the beaver, the turkey, etc., etc.—I cannot but feel as if I lived in a tamed, and, as it were, emasculated country.

I take infinite pains to know all the phenomena of spring, for instance, thinking that I have the entire poem, and then to my chagrin, I hear that it is but an imperfect copy that I possess and have read, that my ancestors have torn out many of the first leaves and grandest passages, and mutilated it in many places.

JOURNAL, *March 23, 1856*

Our village life would stagnate if it were not for the unexplored forests and meadows which surround it. We need the tonic of wildness— to wade sometimes in marshes where the bittern and the meadow-hen lurk, and hear the booming of the snipe; to smell the whispering sedge where only some wilder and more solitary fowl builds her nest, and the mink crawls with its belly close to the ground.

WALDEN, *Spring*

Each town should have a park, or rather a primitive forest of five hundred or a thousand acres, where a stick should never be cut for fuel, a common possession forever, for instruction and recreation.

JOURNAL, *October 15, 1859*

Most men, it seems to me, do not care for Nature and would sell their share in all her beauty, as long as they may live, for a stated sum—many for a glass of rum. Thank God, men cannot as yet fly, and lay waste the sky as well as the earth! We are safe on that side for the present. It is for the very reason that some do not care for those things that we need to continue to protect all from the vandalism of a few.

JOURNAL, *January 3, 1861*

The era of the Wild Apple will soon be past. It is a fruit which will probably become extinct in New England. . . . I fear that he who walks over these fields a century hence will not know the pleasure of knocking off wild apples. Ah, poor man, there are many pleasures which he will not know!

WILD APPLES, *1862*

There is a higher law affecting our relation to pines as well as to men. A pine cut down, a dead pine, is no more a pine than a dead human carcass is a man. Can he who has discovered only some of the values of whalebone and whale oil be said to have discovered the true use of the whale? Can he who slays the elephant for his ivory be said to have "seen the elephant"?

Every creature is better alive than dead, men and moose and pine trees, and he who understands it aright will rather preserve its life than destroy it.

The very willow-rows lopped every three years for fuel and powder, and every sizable pine or oak, or other forest tree, cut down within the memory of man! As if individual speculators were to be allowed to export the clouds out of the sky, or the stars out of the firmament one by one.

THE MAINE WOODS, *Chesuncook, 1864*

It concerns us all whether these proprietors choose to cut down all the woods this winter or not.

JOURNAL, *January 22, 1852*

They have cut down two or three of the very rare celtis trees, not found anywhere else in town. The Lord deliver us from these vandalic proprietors!

If some are prosecuted for abusing children, others deserve to be prosecuted for maltreating the face of nature committed to their care.

JOURNAL, *September 28, 1857*

What is the use of a house if you haven't got a tolerable planet to put it on?

LETTER TO HARRISON BLAKE, *May 20, 1860*

At the same time that we are earnest to explore and learn all things we require that all things be mysterious and unexplorable, that land and sea be infinitely wild, unsurveyed and unfathomed by us because unfathomable. We can never have enough of nature.

WALDEN, *Spring*

The seashore is a sort of neutral ground, a most advantageous point from which to contemplate this world. . . . The waves forever rolling to the land are too far-traveled and untamable to be familiar.

Though once there were more whales cast up here, I think that it was never more wild than now. We do not associate the idea of antiquity with the ocean, nor wonder how it looked a thousand years ago, as we do of the land, for it was equally wild and unfathomable always. . . . The aspect of the shore only has changed. The ocean is a wilderness reaching round the globe. . . . Serpents, bears, hyenas, tigers, rapidly vanish as civilization advances, but the most populous and civilized city cannot scare a shark far from its wharves.

CAPE COD, *The Sea and the Desert, 1855*

Life consists with wildness. The most alive is the wildest.

We go eastward to realize history and study the works of art and literature, retracing the steps of the race; we go westward as into the future, with a spirit of enterprise and adventure.

The West of which I speak is but another name for the Wild; and what I have been preparing to say is, that in Wildness is the preservation of the World.

WALKING, *1862*

2

Technology

"Men have become the tools of their tools."

JOURNAL, *1845*

Our inventions are wont to be pretty toys which distract our attention from serious things. They are but improved means to an unimproved end, an end which it was already but too easy to arrive at; as railroads lead to Boston or New York.

The improvements of ages have had but little influence on the essential laws of man's existence; as our skeletons, probably, are not to be distinguished from those of our ancestors.

WALDEN, *Economy*

The nation itself, with all its so-called internal improvements, which, by the way are all external and superficial, is . . . an unwieldy and overgrown establishment, cluttered with furniture and tripped up by its own traps, ruined by luxury and heedless expense, by want of calculation and a worthy aim, as the million households in the land; and the only cure for it, as for them, is in a rigid economy, a stern and more than spartan simplicity of life and elevation of purpose.

Men think that it is essential that the *Nation* have commerce, and export ice, and talk through a telegraph, and ride thirty miles an hour, without a doubt, whether *they* do or not, but whether we should live like baboons or like men, is a little uncertain.

We do not ride upon the railroad; it rides upon us.

WALDEN, *What I Lived For*

We are in great haste to construct a magnetic telegraph from Maine to Texas; but Maine and Texas, it may be, have nothing important to communicate. . . . We are eager to tunnel under the Atlantic and bring the Old World some weeks nearer to the New; but perchance the first news that will leak through into the broad flapping American ear will be that the Princess Adelaide has the whooping cough.

WALDEN, *Economy*

Only make something to take the place of something, and men will behave as if it was the very thing they wanted.

A WEEK, *Monday*

Almost all our improvements, so called, tend to convert the country into the town.

JOURNAL, *August 22, 1860*

While civilization has been improving our houses, it has not equally improved the men who are to inhabit them. It has created palaces, but it was not so easy to create noblemen and kings.

WALDEN, *Economy*

3

Livelihood

"It is remarkable that there is little or nothing to be remembered written on the subject of getting a living; how to make getting a living not merely honest and honorable, but altogether inviting and glorious; for if getting a living is not so, then living is not."

LIFE WITHOUT PRINCIPLE, *1863*

I have travelled a good deal in Concord; and everywhere, in shops, and offices, and fields, the inhabitants have appeared to me to be doing penance in a thousand remarkable ways. . . . The twelve labors of Hercules were trifling in comparison with those which my neighbors have undertaken; for they were only twelve and had an end; but I could never see that these men slew or captured any monster or finished any labor.

Actually, the laboring man has not leisure for a true integrity day by day; he cannot afford to sustain the manliest relations to men; his labor would be depreciated in the market. He has no time to be anything but a machine. How can he remember well his ignorance—which his growth requires—who has so often to use his knowledge?

WALDEN, *Economy*

I have no doubt that some of you who read this book are unable to pay for all the dinners which you have actually eaten, or for the coats and shoes which are fast wearing or are already worn out, and have come to this page to spend borrowed or stolen time, robbing your creditors of an hour. . . . Always on the limits, trying to get into business and trying to get out of debt.

WALDEN, *Economy*

Let not to get a living be thy trade, but thy sport. Enjoy the land, but own it not. Through want of enterprise and faith men are where they are, buying and selling, and spending their lives like serfs.

WALDEN, *Baker Farm*

It is hard to have a Southern overseer; it is worse to have a Northern one; but worst of all when you are the slave-driver of yourself.

WALDEN, *Economy*

Let us consider the way in which we spend our lives. This world is a place of business. What an infinite bustle! I am awaked almost every night by the panting of the locomotive. It interrupts my dreams. There is no sabbath. It would be glorious to see mankind at leisure for once. It is nothing but work, work, work.

To have done anything by which you earned money *merely* is to have been truly idle or worse.

The aim of the laborer should be, not to get his living, to get "a good job," but to perform well a certain work; and, even in a pecuniary sense, it would be economy for a town to pay its laborers so well that they would not feel that they were working for low ends, as for a livelihood merely, but for scientific, or even moral ends. Do not hire a man who does your work for money, but him who does it for love of it.

There is no more fatal blunderer than he who consumes the greater part of his life getting his living. All great enterprises are self-supporting; the poet, for instance, must sustain his body by his poetry, as a steam plowing-mill feeds its boilers with the shavings it makes. You must get your living by loving.

LIFE WITHOUT PRINCIPLE, *1863*

For more than five years I maintained myself thus solely by the labor of my hands, and I found that, by working about six weeks in a year, I could meet all the expenses of living.

WALDEN, *Economy*

If I should sell both my forenoons and afternoons to society, as most appear to do, I am sure that for me there would be nothing left worth living for. I trust that I shall never thus sell my birthright for a mess of pottage. I wish to suggest that a man may be very industrious, and yet not spend his time well.

The ways in which most men get their living, that is, live, are mere makeshifts, and a shirking of the real business of life—chiefly because they do not know, but partly because they do not mean, any better.

LIFE WITHOUT PRINCIPLE, *1863*

It is not necessary that a man should earn his living by the sweat of his brow, unless he sweats easier than I do.

The life which men praise and regard as successful is but one kind. Why should we exaggerate any one kind at the expense of the others?

WALDEN, *Economy*

4

Living

"I went to the woods because I wished to live deliberately, to front only the essential facts of life, and see if I could not learn what it had to teach, and not, when I came to die, discover that I had not lived."

WALDEN, *What I Lived For*

One young man of my acquaintance, who has inherited some acres, told me that he thought he should live as I did, *if he had the means.* I would not have anyone adopt *my* mode of living on any account; for, beside that before he has fairly learned it I may have found out another for myself, I desire that there be as many different persons in the world as possible; but I would have each one be very careful to find out and pursue *his own* way, and not his father's or his mother's or his neighbor's instead.

WALDEN, *Economy*

A man cannot be said to succeed in this life
who does not satisfy one friend.

JOURNAL, *February 19, 1857*

To affect the quality of the days, that is the
highest of the arts. Every man is tasked to
make his life, even in its details, worthy of the
contemplation of his most elevated and critical
hour.

Our life is frittered away by detail. . . . Simplicity, simplicity, simplicity! I say, let your
affairs be as two or three, and not a hundred
or a thousand; instead of a million count half
a dozen, and keep your accounts on your
thumbnail.

WALDEN, *What I Lived For*

The mass of men lead lives of quiet desperation. What is called resignation is confirmed
desperation. From the desperate city you go
into the desperate country, and have to console
yourself with the bravery of minks and musk-
rats. A stereotyped but unconscious despair

is concealed even under what are called the games and amusements of mankind. There is no play in them, for this comes after work. But it is a characteristic of wisdom not to do desperate things.

When we consider what, to use the words of the catechism, is the chief end of man, and what are the true necessaries and means of life, it appears as if men had deliberately chosen the common mode of living because they preferred it to any other. Yet they honestly think there is no choice left. But alert and healthy natures remember that the sun rose clear. It is never too late to give up our prejudices. No way of thinking or doing, however ancient, can be trusted without proof.

WALDEN, *Economy*

What is the pill which will keep us well, serene, contented? . . . For my panacea, instead of one of those quack vials of a mixture dipped from Acheron and the Dead Sea . . . let me have a draught of undiluted morning air.

Morning air! If men will not drink of this at the fountainhead of the day, why, then, we must even bottle up some and sell it in the shops, for the benefit of those who have lost their subscription ticket to morning time in this world.

WALDEN, *Solitude*

I think that I cannot preserve my health and spirits, unless I spend four hours a day at least—and it is commonly more than that—sauntering through the woods and over the hills and fields, absolutely free from all worldly engagements.

The mechanics and shopkeepers stay in their shops not only all the forenoon, but all the afternoon, too, sitting with crossed legs, so many of them—as if the legs were made to sit upon, and not to stand or walk upon—I think that they deserve some credit for not having all committed suicide long ago.

The walking of which I speak has nothing in it akin to taking exercise, as it is called, as the sick take medicine at stated hours—as the swinging of dumbbells or chairs; but is itself the enterprise and adventure of the day. If you would get exercise, go in search of the springs of life. Think of a man's swinging dumbbells for his health, when those springs are bubbling up in far-off pastures unsought by him!

Of course it is of no use to direct our steps to the woods, if they do not carry us thither. I am alarmed when it happens that I have walked a mile into the woods bodily, without getting there in spirit.

WALKING, 1862

If you would know the flavor of huckleberries, ask the cow-boy or the partridge. It is a vulgar error to suppose that you have tasted huckleberries who never plucked them. . . . The ambrosial and essential part of the fruit is lost with the bloom which is rubbed off in the market cart, and they become mere provender.

WALDEN, *The Ponds*

He will be regarded as a benefactor of his race who shall teach man to confine himself to a more innocent and wholesome diet. Whatever my own practice may be, I have no doubt that it is a part of the destiny of the human race, in its gradual improvement, to leave off eating animals.

I believe that every man who has ever been earnest to preserve his higher or poetic faculties in the best condition has been particularly inclined to abstain from animal food, and from much food of any kind.

WALDEN, *Higher Laws*

Why concern ourselves so much about our beans for seed, and not be concerned at all about a new generation of men?

WALDEN, *The Bean-Field*

Let us settle ourselves, and work and wedge our feet downward through the mud and slush of opinion, and prejudice, and tradition, and delusion, and appearance, that alluvion which covers the globe, through Paris and London, through New York and Boston and Concord, through Church and State, through poetry and philosophy and religion, till we come to a hard bottom and rocks in place, which we can call *reality*, and say, This is, and no mistake. . . . Be it life or death, we crave only reality. . . . If we are alive, let us go about our business.

WALDEN, *What I Lived For*

What is a course of history or philosophy, or poetry, no matter how well selected, or the best society, or the most admirable routine of life, compared with the discipline of looking always at what is to be seen? Will you be a reader, a student merely, or a seer? Read your fate, see what is before you, and walk on into futurity.

WALDEN, *Sounds*

Why level downward to our dullest perception always, and praise that as common sense? The commonest sense is the sense of men asleep, which they express by snoring.

WALDEN, *Conclusion*

We spend more on almost any article of bodily aliment [nourishment] or ailment than on our mental aliment. It is time that we had un-common schools, that we did not leave off our education when we begin to be men and women.

WALDEN, *Reading*

What everybody echoes or in silence passes by as true today may turn out to be falsehood to-morrow, mere smoke of opinion. . . . What old people say you cannot do, you try and find that you can. Old deeds for old people, and new deeds for new.

WALDEN, *Economy*

The fate of the country . . . does not depend on what kind of paper you drop into the ballot-box once a year, but on what kind of man you drop from your chamber into the street every morning.

SLAVERY IN MASSACHUSETTS, *1854*

I think that we should be men first, and subjects afterward. It is not desirable to cultivate a respect for the law, so much as for the right.

CIVIL DISOBEDIENCE, *1849*

The law will never make men free; it is men who have got to make the law free. They are the lovers of law and order who observe the law when the government breaks it.

SLAVERY IN MASSACHUSETTS, *1854*

I am convinced, that if all men were to live as simply as I then did, thieving and robbery would be unknown. These take place only in communities where some have got more than is sufficient while others have not enough.

WALDEN, *The Village*

I left the woods for as good a reason as I went there. Perhaps it seemed to me that I had several more lives to live, and could not spare any more time for that one.

WALDEN, *Conclusion*

5

Possessions

"A man is rich in proportion to the number of things he can afford to let alone."

WALDEN, *What I Lived For*

It would be some advantage to live a primitive and frontier life, though in the midst of an outward civilization, if only to learn what are the gross necessaries of life and what methods have been taken to obtain them; or even to look over the old day-books of the merchants, to see what it was that men most commonly bought at the stores, what they stored, that is, what are the grossest groceries.

The necessaries of life for man in this climate may, accurately enough, be distributed under the several heads of Food, Shelter, Clothing, and Fuel; for not till we have secured these are we prepared to entertain the true problems of life with freedom and a prospect of success.

By proper Shelter and Clothing we legitimately retain our own internal heat, but with an excess of these, or of Fuel, that is, with an external heat greater than our own internal, may not cookery properly be said to begin?

When a man is warmed by the several modes which I have described, what does he want next? Surely not more warmth of the same kind, as more and richer food, larger and more splendid houses, finer and more abundant clothing, more numerous, incessant, and hotter fires, and the like.

Shall we always study to obtain more of these things, and not sometimes to be content with less?

WALDEN, *Economy*

Do not trouble yourself much to get new things, whether clothes or friends. Turn the old; return to them. Things do not change; we change. Sell your clothes and keep your thoughts.

WALDEN, *Conclusion*

No man ever stood the lower in my estimation for having a patch in his clothes; yet I am sure that there is greater anxiety, commonly, to have fashionable, or at least clean and un-patched clothes, than to have a sound con-science. . . . Most behave as if they believed that their prospects for life would be ruined if they should do it. It would be easier for them to hobble to town with a broken leg than with a broken pantaloon.

I say, beware of all enterprises that require new clothes, and not rather a new wearer of clothes. If there is not a new man, how can the new clothes be made to fit? If you have any en-terprise before you, try it in your old clothes.

WALDEN, *Economy*

In my experience I have found nothing so truly impoverishing as what is called wealth, i.e., the command of greater means than you had before possessed, though comparatively few and slight still, for you thus inevitably ac-quire a more expensive habit of living, and

41

even the very same necessaries and comforts cost you more than they once did. Instead of gaining, you have lost some independence, and if your income should be suddenly lessened, you would find yourself poor, though possessed of the same means which once made you rich.

JOURNAL, *January 20, 1856*

And when the farmer has got his house, he may not be the richer but the poorer for it, and it be the house that has got him.

Most of the luxuries, and many of the so-called comforts of life, are not only not indispensable, but positive hindrances to the elevation of mankind. With respect to luxuries and comforts, the wisest have even lived a more simple and meagre life than the poor.

WALDEN, *Economy*

That man is the richest whose pleasures are the cheapest.

JOURNAL, *March 11, 1856*

6

Time

"Above all, we cannot afford not to live in the present. He is blessed over all mortals who loses no moment of the passing life in remembering the past."

WALKING, *1862*

In any weather, at any hour of the day or night, I have been anxious to improve the nick of time, and notch it on my stick, too; to stand on the meeting of two eternities, the past and future, which is precisely the present moment.

WALDEN, *Economy*

Let us spend one day as deliberately as Nature, and not be thrown off the track by every nutshell and mosquito's wing that falls on the rails. . . . If the engine whistles, let it whistle till it is hoarse for its pains. If the bell rings, why should we run?

Why should we live with such hurry and waste of life?

WALDEN, *What I Lived For*

As if you could kill time without injuring eternity.

WALDEN, *Economy*

Many a forenoon have I stolen away, preferring to spend thus the most valued part of the day; for I was rich, if not in money, in sunny hours and summer days, and spent them lavishly.

WALDEN, *The Ponds*

I love a broad margin to my life. Sometimes, in a summer morning, having taken my accustomed bath, I sat in my sunny doorway from sunrise to noon, rapt in a revery, amidst the pines and hickories and sumachs, in undisturbed solitude and stillness. . . . I grew in those seasons like corn in the night, and they were far better than any work of the hands

would have been. They were not time sub-
tracted from my life, but so much over and
above my usual allowance.

My days were not days of the week, bearing
the stamp of any heathen deity, nor were they
minced into hours and fretted by the ticking of
a clock; for I lived like the Puri Indians of
whom it is said that "for yesterday, today, and
tomorrow they have only one word, and they
express the variety of meaning by pointing
backward for yesterday, forward for tomorrow, and overhead for the passing day."

WALDEN, *Sounds*

In eternity there is indeed something true and
sublime. But all those times and places and oc-
casions are now and here. God himself cul-
minates in the present moment, and will never
be more divine in the lapse of all the ages.

WALDEN, *What I Lived For*

We should be blessed if we lived in the present
always, and took advantage of every accident

that befell us. . . . We loiter in winter while it
is already spring.

WALDEN, *Spring*

The startings and arrivals of the [railway] cars
. . . go and come with such regularity and pre-
cision, and their whistle can be heard so far,
that the farmers set their clocks by them, and
thus one well-conducted institution regulates a
whole country. Have not men improved some-
what in punctuality since the railroad was in-
vented? Do not they talk and think faster in the
depot than they did in the stage-office?

WALDEN, *Sounds*

Nothing can be more useful to a man than a
determination not to be hurried.

JOURNAL, *March 22, 1842*

Time is but the stream I go a-fishing in. I drink
at it; but while I drink I see the sandy bottom
and detect how shallow it is. Its thin current
slides away, but eternity remains.

WALDEN, *What I Lived For*

7

Aspiration

"I found in myself, and still find, an instinct toward a higher, or, as it is named, spiritual life, as do most men, and another toward a primitive rank and savage one, and I reverence them both. I love the wild not less than the good."

WALDEN, *Higher Laws*

Heaven is under our feet as well as over our heads.

WALDEN, *The Pond in Winter*

Be a Columbus to whole new continents and worlds within you, opening new channels, not of trade, but of thought.

The Universe is wider than our views of it.

WALDEN, *Conclusion*

In proportion as our inward life fails, we go more constantly and desperately to the post office. You may depend on it, that the poor fellow who walks away with the greatest number of letters, proud of his extensive correspondence, has not heard from himself this long while.

LIFE WITHOUT PRINCIPLE, *1863*

We are accustomed to say in New England that few and fewer pigeons visit us every year. Our forests furnish no mast for them. So, it would seem, few and fewer thoughts visit each growing man from year to year, for the grove in our minds is laid waste. . . . Our winged thoughts are turned to poultry. They no longer soar.

We hug the earth—how rarely we mount! Me thinks we might elevate ourselves a little more. We might climb a tree, at least.

The wildest dreams of wild men, even, are not the less true, though they may not recommend themselves to the sense which is most common among Englishmen and Americans today. It is not every truth that recommends itself to the common sense.

WALKING, *1862*

What a man thinks of himself, that it is which determines, or rather indicates, his fate.

But man's capacities have never been measured; nor are we to judge of what he can do by any precedents, so little has been tried.

WALDEN, *Economy*

I know of no more encouraging fact than the unquestionable ability of man to elevate his life by a conscious endeavor.

WALDEN, *What I Lived For*

If one advances confidently in the direction of his dreams, and endeavors to live the life which he has imagined, he will meet with a success unexpected in common hours.

If you have built castles in the air, your work need not be lost; that is where they should be. Now put the foundations under them.

WALDEN, *Conclusion*

Goodness is the only investment that never fails.

WALDEN, *Higher Laws*

Why should we be in such desperate haste to succeed and in such desperate enterprises? If a man does not keep pace with his companions, perhaps it is because he hears a different drummer. Let him step to the music which he hears, however measured or far away.

WALDEN, *Conclusion*

I think that we may safely trust a good deal more than we do. We may waive just so much care of ourselves as we honestly bestow elsewhere. Nature is as well adapted to our weakness as to our strength.

In the long run, men hit only what they aim at.

WALDEN, *Economy*

No face which we can give to a matter will stead us so well at last as truth. This alone wears well.

WALDEN, *Conclusion*

To be a philosopher is not merely to have subtle thoughts, nor even to found a school, but so to love wisdom as to live according to its dictates, a life of simplicity, independence, magnanimity and trust. It is to solve some of the problems of life, not only theoretically, but practically.

WALDEN, *Economy*

I have always been regretting that I was not as wise as the day I was born.

WALDEN, *What I Lived For*

No man ever followed his genius till it misled him. . . . If the day and night are such you greet them with joy, and life emits a fragrance like flowers and sweet-scented herbs, is more elastic, more starry, more immortal—that is your success.

Every man is the builder of a temple, called his body, to the god he worships, after a style purely his own—nor can he get off by hammering marble instead. We are all sculptors and painters, and our material is our own flesh and blood and bones. Any nobleness begins at once to refine a man's features, any meanness or sensuality to imbrute them.

WALDEN, *Higher Laws*

Rather than love, than money, than fame, give me truth. I sat at a table where were rich food and wine in abundance . . . but sincerity and truth were not; and I went away hungry from the inhospitable board. . . . There was a man in my neighborhood who lived in a hollow tree. His manners were truly regal. I should have done better had I called on him.

WALDEN, *Conclusion*

John Farmer sat at his door one September evening, after a hard day's work, his mind still running on his labor more or less. . . . He had not attended to the train of his thoughts long when he heard someone playing on a flute and that sound harmonized with his mood. . . . The notes of the flute came home to his ears out of a different sphere from that he worked in, and suggested work for certain faculties which slumbered in him. They gently did away with the street, and the village, and the state in which he lived.

A voice said to him—Why do you stay here and live this mean moiling life, when a glorious existence is possible for you? Those same stars twinkle over other fields than these. But how to come out of this condition and actually migrate thither? All that he could think of was to practice some new austerity, to let his mind descend into his body and redeem

it, and treat himself with ever increasing respect.

WALDEN, Higher Laws

The life in us is like the water in the river. It
may rise this year higher than man has ever
known it, and flood the parched uplands.

Only that day dawns to which we are awake.
There is more day to dawn. The sun is but a
morning star.

WALDEN, Conclusion

About the Author

Henry David Thoreau was born on July 12, 1817, in Concord, Massachusetts, where he lived for most of his life except for brief sojourns out of state and to Canada. Educated at Harvard, he returned home to Concord, and supported himself in diverse ways—in the family pencil-making business, and as handyman, teacher, lecturer, and surveyor.

On July 4, 1845, Thoreau decided to move to Walden Pond, on the outskirts of Concord, where he built a cabin in the woods, remaining there for a little over two years. He recounted his experience in essential living in *Walden; or, Life in the Woods*, published in 1854, seven years after leaving Walden Pond.

Thoreau is not only one of the greatest American authors, but commands a major place in world literature as well; his works have been translated into virtually every modern language. He wrote many books and essays, in addition to his voluminous *Journal* from which he drew much of the material for his other works. Thoreau died in Concord of tuberculosis, on May 6, 1862.

About the Editor

Carol Spenard LaRusso is an executive editor at New World Library and has been with the publishing house since 1981. She has taught English and music, and has a B.A. and M.A. in English literature. Born and raised in New York, she moved to San Francisco in 1968, and currently makes her home in Marin County, California, near her two daughters and grand-daughters.

Bibliographic Notes

The standard edition of Thoreau's complete works is the 20-volume set published in 1906 by Houghton Mifflin. Thoreau's books, essays, and his multi-volume *Journal* have been published in numerous editions and collections. Many biographies and collections of correspondence and criticism are also available. Below is a partial list of Thoreau's works, some of which were published posthumously.

BOOKS

A Week on the Concord and Merrimack Rivers, 1849
Walden; or, Life in the Woods, 1854
The Maine Woods, 1864
Cape Cod, 1865
A Yankee in Canada, 1866

Essays

On the Duty of Civil Disobedience, 1849
Slavery in Massachusetts, 1854
A Plea for Captain John Brown, 1860
Wild Apples, 1860
Walking, 1862
Life Without Principle, 1863

THE CLASSIC WISDOM COLLECTION
OF
NEW WORLD LIBRARY

As You Think by James Allen. Edited and with an Introduction by Marc Allen. October, 1991.

Native American Wisdom. Compiled and with an Introduction by Kent Nerburn and Louise Mengelkoch. October, 1991.

The Art of True Healing by Israel Regardie. Edited and updated by Marc Allen. October, 1991.

Letters to a Young Poet by Rainer Maria Rilke. Translated by Joan M. Burnham with an Introduction by Marc Allen. April, 1992.

The Green Thoreau. Selected and with an Introduction by Carol Spenard LaRusso. April, 1992.

The Message of a Master by John McDonald. Edited and with an Introduction by Katherine Dieter. April, 1992.

New World Library is dedicated to publishing books and cassettes that help improve the quality of our lives.

For a catalog of our fine books and cassettes, contact:

New World Library
58 Paul Drive
San Rafael, CA 94903
Phone: (415) 472-2100
FAX: (415) 472-6131

Or call toll free:

(800) 227-3900
In Calif.: (800) 632-2122